ENVIRONMENTAL DISASTERS

By Shirley Duke

ROURKE
PUBLISHING

www.rourkepublishing.com

www.rourkepublishing.com

PHOTO CREDITS: Cover © Wikipedia; Title Page © United States Coast Guard, wim class, Rechitan Sorin, Huguette Roe; Table of Credits © Mark Smith; Page 4 © United States Coast Guard; Page 5 © Alyssia Sheikh; Page 6 © U.S. Fish and Wildlife Service; Page 7 © wim claes, Alyssia Sheikh; Page 8 © Jessica Nelson; Page 9 © U.S. Fish and Wildlife Service; Page 10 © Christian Lopetz; Page 11 © Danny E Hooks, Pete Souza official White House photographer; Page 12 © Péter Gudella, Alyssia Sheikh; Page 13 © Mark Winfrey, ©EPA; Page 15 © Coolcaesar; Page 16 © Huguette Roe, Stephen Gibson, Alyssia Sheikh; Page 17 © Pan Xunbin, Rob Byron; Page 18 © Photoroller; Page 19 © Orietta Gaspari, Alyssia Sheikh; Page 20 © whitewizzard; Page 21 © Emel Yenigelen; Page 22 © Alex Ciopata, Andrea Danti; Page 23 © Dobresum, Alyssia Sheikh; Page 24 © axyse; Page 25 © Marque1313, courtesy of United States Federal Government; Page 26 © Emir Simsek, Christian Lopetz Page 27 © Nomad_Soul, Alyssia Sheikh; Page 28 © Sergey Kamshylin, Iryna Rasko; Page 29 © photocell; Page 30/31 © Mark Smith; Page 31 © Dannyphoto80; Page 32 © Lilac Mountain; Page 33 © 3355m; Page 34 © steveball; Page 35 © jiawangkun; Page 36 © NOAA; Page 37 © NASA, NOAA, Page 38/39 © Denton Rumsey; Page 38 © Triff; Page 39 © Borislav Toskov; Page 40/41 © mikeledray Page 40 © NOAA; Page 42 © Aaron Kohr, Olegusk; Page 43 © Jan Martin Will, artiomp; Page 44 © Eric Isselée; Page 45 © NOAA, Undersea Discoveries,

Edited by Precious McKenzie

Cover design by Teri Intzegian
Layout by Blue Door Publishing, Florida

Library of Congress Cataloging-in-Publication Data

Duke, Shirley
 Environmental Disasters / Shirley Duke
  p. cm. -- (Let's Explore Science)
 ISBN 978-1-61741-784-9 (hard cover) (alk. paper)
 ISBN 978-1-61741-986-7 (soft cover)
 Library of Congress Control Number: 2011924829

Rourke Publishing
Printed in the United States of America, North Mankato, Minnesota
060711
060711CL

ROURKE PUBLISHING

www.rourkepublishing.com - rourke@rourkepublishing.com
Post Office Box 643328 Vero Beach, Florida 32964

Table of Contents

CHAPTER ONE

Oil Spill

In 2010 an explosion shattered a quiet April evening in the Gulf of Mexico. Flames roared into the air on the Deepwater Horizon offshore oil platform. Startled workers scrambled to escape. Most of them reached safety. Millions of gallons of light crude oil gushed from the site.

On April 22, 2010, the Deepwater Horizon sank. Oil poured into Gulf waters.

Drilling for oil over water required floating platforms that resembled barges. Early offshore drilling stayed on the ocean floor in shallower water. Later, platforms with supports reaching to the ocean floor held the equipment and workers. Then new technology made oil drilling in the deep ocean profitable. Oil rigs supported the giant platforms and the production crews necessary for deep water drilling. Companies rushed to lease Gulf coast sites. The huge Deepwater Horizon was designed to drill in 7,000 feet (2.1 kilometers) of water.

A blowout preventer, a valve that closes off and covers the bore hole if it blows out, hadn't stopped the explosion. The well's depth made stopping the oil flow more difficult. British Petroleum (BP) worked to plug the leak. Workers drilled relief wells and capped the leak. But for eighty-six days, the well poured over 185 million gallons (700 million liters) of oil into the Gulf. This spill dwarfed the 11 million gallon (41 million liters) spill of the *Exxon Valdez* tanker in 1989 along the Alaskan coast.

Georgia

Alabama

Mississippi

Florida

Louisiana

Gulf of Mexico

oil spill

Biologists from the U.S. Fish and Wildlife Department worked to rescue birds from the oil spill.

Wildlife lived on Gulf beaches, deltas, barrier islands, marshes, and the deep ocean floor. Oil affected life at every level. Gushing oil made plumes in the open water. Waves and currents broke apart the plumes. Smaller oil blobs floated free in the water. For a month, the oil floated in the Gulf. Then lines of oil arrived with the waves, coating whatever life it reached. Marshes and wetlands in Louisiana were hit first. The oil moved across the coasts of Mississippi, Alabama, and Florida. The oil also drifted down to the ocean floor.

Clean-up began immediately. The U.S. government holds the driller responsible for cleaning up the spill. Clean-up crews and volunteers from across the country rescued oil-covered animals and worked to collect the oil. Scientists feared the immediate danger and worried about the future of the Gulf coast.

The *Exxon Valdez* accident taught lessons on oil spills and oil removal. There, oil coated 1,300 miles (2,000 kilometers) of Alaskan coastline. The images of oily animals shocked people. The spill killed hundreds of thousands of birds, otters, seals, eagles, whales, and billions of salmon and herring eggs. Oil remains on some beaches today.

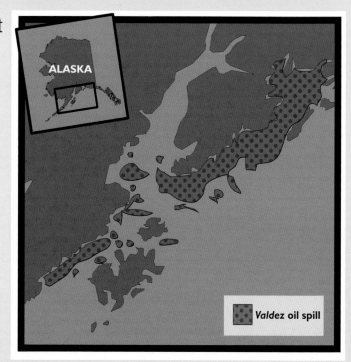

ALASKA

Valdez oil spill

Oil and Birds

Effects of an oil spill on birds shows up right away. But other problems can occur, too. Oil damages feathers. With damaged feathers birds can't float or fly. They try to clean their feathers and the oil poisons them. They lose their insulating ability. Birds get cold and die.

Oil-coated food is harmful, too. Liver damage or blindness from eating oil keeps animals from competing for food or escaping predators. Long term, oil affects organs, changes behavior, and damages genes.

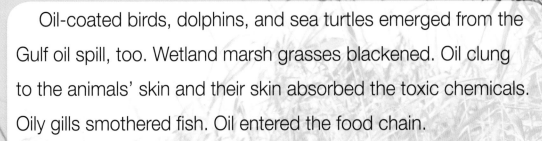

Oil-coated birds, dolphins, and sea turtles emerged from the Gulf oil spill, too. Wetland marsh grasses blackened. Oil clung to the animals' skin and their skin absorbed the toxic chemicals. Oily gills smothered fish. Oil entered the food chain.

Absorbent pads, skimmers, and booms soaked up or contained the oil for removal. Workers spent months cleaning animals and wiping marsh grasses. Chemical **dispersants** like deodorized kerosene broke apart oil pools.

Long booms float on the water in an attempt to contain the spilled oil from fouling these marshes. The boom has a skirt that hangs below the slick to keep the oil from spreading.

Workers sucked up surface oil from inside floating booms or burned it. Some oil broke into tiny pieces and floated off.

Oil stays in the environment for years. Birds migrate through wetlands. Coastal habitats support eggs and larvae of countless animals. Oiled food and habitats kill billions of eggs and the young of fish and shellfish. Damaged habitats harm endangered or fragile species. The toll of the spill isn't clear yet. Scientists believe it could affect marine life for years.

U.S. Fish and Wildlife biologists dug up sea turtle nests and their eggs along the Gulf Coast. They shipped the eggs to the space center in Florida, saving a generation of hatchlings from swimming into the oil-filled water.

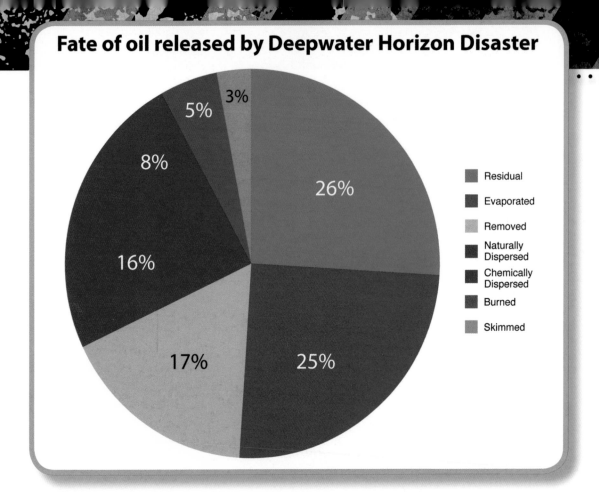

Fate of oil released by Deepwater Horizon Disaster

3%
5%
8%
26%
16%
17%
25%

- Residual
- Evaporated
- Removed
- Naturally Dispersed
- Chemically Dispersed
- Burned
- Skimmed

Bioremediation, where microbes clean oil in the environment, happens in the Gulf naturally. Scientists seeded areas with additional oil-consuming microbes. Some oil remained in the water, depositing lines of oil and tar balls on shore. Building six foot (two meter) high **berms**, or physical barriers, protected wetlands.

The spill affected people, too. Over one billion pounds (453 million kilograms) of fish and shellfish come from the Gulf. Fishing and tourism stopped because of the spill. Commercial fishing and pleasure fishing areas shut down. Many people lost their businesses. They couldn't fish or keep their restaurants and hotels open. With reduced amounts of shrimp and oysters, seafood prices rose in restaurants.

Blobs of oil and tar reached Florida beaches in early June 2010. Oily beaches caused thousands of tourists to cancel their vacation plans to the Gulf coast. The Commerce Secretary declared a fishery disaster for Louisiana, Mississippi, and Alabama.

President Barack Obama

The *Exxon Valdez* spill caused changes in safety regulations. Congress passed the Oil Pollution Act to improve standards. It set standards for spill assessments. For their well spill, BP now had to pay for clean-up.

President Obama revoked his proposal for expanding offshore drilling. He halted current drilling. The president's plan included monitoring oil and seafood. New drilling safety rules were set. No new permits for Gulf drilling will be issued for now.

Deep water drilling is expanding in other parts of the world. But the spill and the subsequent halt to deep water drilling will affect the U.S. for years.

CHAPTER TWO

Solid Waste

The Love Canal

William T. Love planned to build a dream city near Niagara Falls, New York. But financial problems left only a canal. The city dumped waste and industrial chemicals there. In 1942, Hooker Chemical Company bought it and added their wastes. In 1953, Hooker covered the canal with dirt and sold it to the city for $1.00.

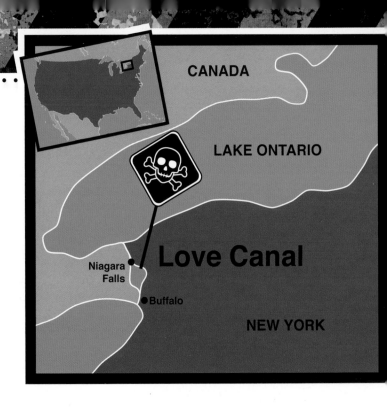

CANADA

LAKE ONTARIO

Love Canal

Niagara Falls

Buffalo

NEW YORK

Thousands of steel barrels like these were buried in the Love Canal. The barrels contained toxic waste.

Soon homes and a school filled the Love Canal community. However, odd odors drifted in. Runoff flooded lawns. Rusty barrels of toxic waste from the former landfill disintegrated. Chemical puddles burned children's hands. Trees and

gardens turned brown. Smelly bubbles floated on the liquids.

By 1978, eighty-two different chemicals had moved upward in the soil. The chemicals soaked yards and basements. Some chemicals were cancer-causing, or **carcinogens**.

Pollutants like herbicides, pesticides, and industrial compounds kill plant and animal life. Waste deposits rich in nitrogen and phosphates can lead to algae overgrowth, which lowers the oxygen levels.

Health changes alarmed the families. Some children had birth defects. People developed nerve disorders. Chemical wastes flowed into the Niagara River. People moved away.

Ninety-eight families relocated and the school closed. By 1978, more than 700 families had to move. President Carter and Congress approved funds to clean up the area. They created the Environmental Protection Agency (EPA) Superfund to force polluters to clean up.

The State of New York and the EPA removed the toxins. Clay seals capped the former canal. After years of legal battles and new laws, the area was declared safe. Homes were built again.

The Love Canal brought attention to hazardous waste. It changed how people viewed the environment. But could a Love Canal happen again?

1960'S	1970'S	1980'S
Rachel Carson's *Silent Spring* book draws attention to the environment.	The Environmental Protection Agency (EPA) is created, consolidating many agencies into one to protect human health and to safeguard the natural environment—air, water, and land.	The Superfund Law passes to clean up old, abandoned waste sites.
The word conservation is replaced by ecology as people grew concerned about air and water pollution.	The U.S. Congress passes the Clean Water Act and Clean Air Act.	EPA begins emergency response planning. States run their own hazardous waste programs.

EPA (Environmental Protection Agency) headquarters is located in Washington D.C.

1990'S

The Clean Air Act Amendment sets limits for dust and soot.

Focus turns to preventing pollution.

2000'S

Improvements in mercury emissions and visibility improves air quality.

EPA responds to September 11, 2001.

Clean diesel engines cut emissions in trucks, buses, and equipment.

Guiyu, China

Heavy smoke and a sharp taste of metal fill the air in Guiyu, China. Small, family-run businesses recycle used electronics. Thousands work at home removing valuable silver and gold from discarded electronics called **e-waste**. Safe recycling reuses the materials in e-waste. But in Guiyu, people pull wires from computers or pour acid over electronic parts to remove the silver and gold. They burn circuit boards and plastics. They pry open printer cartridges and break apart lead-filled computer monitors.

Electronic waste, or post-consumer waste, is growing. With new technology, the old equipment must go somewhere. In the U.S., the EPA controls electronic waste disposal. But proper disposal is ten times more expensive at home than exporting it. Up to 80 percent of all electronic waste comes from the U.S. China allows the import of plastic and scrap metal waste.

Metals like lead, nickel, cadmium, and mercury pose health risks. Improper handling and disposal lets toxic materials leak in landfills. Ash from burned waste is dumped in the waterways. Guiyu trucks in drinking water because theirs is too polluted to drink. Children show high lead levels in their blood. Rashes and breathing problems are common. Long term damage concerns people.

A number of Guiyu residents who work with e-waste are developing skin damage, headaches, dizziness, nausea, stomach problems, and nerve damage. Children are especially at risk.

17

China recycles legally, but families make more money on their own. Waste sits next to rice paddies and fish in local ponds. India, Brazil, and Mexico face similar problems as their electronic waste rises. The problem is growing worldwide.

Many companies recycle e-waste. Still, tons of electronics go to places like China, India, or Africa. The EPA and environmentalists hope to get a bill passed banning all exports of electronic wastes. Recycling electronics saves money, energy, and reduces landfills while saving the environment, if it is done properly.

Drop off used electronics like computers, laptops, cell phones, TVs, copiers, fax machines, and monitors at a trusted recycling center. Safe, quality recycling will not put e-waste into landfills.

The Oceans

In the northern Pacific, ocean currents come together. They collide to form a slowly rotating mass, or **gyre**. This particular gyre has a great accumulation of trash—mostly plastics. The circling trash has no exact form or location. The media named the area the Great Pacific Garbage Dump.

The mass of trash floats just below the surface. Scientists dispute the actual size, but they agree plastic litter has no place in the ocean. Fishing nets, toys, syringes, cigarette lighters, combs, plastic bags, and bottle caps swirl around millions of tiny plastic pieces.

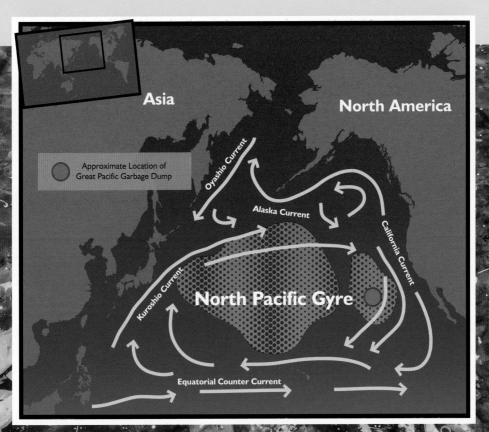

Asia

North America

Approximate Location of
Great Pacific Garbage Dump

Oyashio Current

Alaska Current

California Current

Kuroshio Current

North Pacific Gyre

Equatorial Counter Current

Plastic makes up around 90 percent of all ocean debris. The rest is biodegradable. Plastics break apart but hold their chemical bonds. Sun exposure and friction against the waves create small pieces.

Scientists worry about marine life. Mistaking plastic for food kills countless seabirds and marine mammals. Toothbrushes, syringes, and lighters have been found in the stomachs of dead birds. When marine life **ingests** plastics, they ingest toxins the plastics may have absorbed from the contaminated water. Ingesting plastics affects the food chain by putting toxins into human food sources.

Parent birds mistaking plastic pellets for food carry them back to their chicks and feed it to them. The chicks choke, starve, or die from being unable to digest the plastic.

Some plastics come from oil rigs and ships. Most comes from land. Water washing across Southeast Asia, North America, Canada and Mexico carries trash to the oceans. Currents move the trash along. Research on oceans and plastic waste is in the early stages.

Toxic chemicals, post-consumer waste, and plastics are part of life in the twenty-first century. What people do and how they make changes concerning those problems will determine the future for Earth's oceans.

Plastics

In 1909, a Belgian chemist invented a hard, moldable material never before made—plastic! He called it Bakelite and it made him rich. Chemists experimented and before long, nylon, foam rubber, and Plexiglas were common. Clear plastic wrap kept food fresh longer. By 1957, single use plastic bags appeared. Bottled water entered the marketplace. From buttons to cars, plastics are everywhere. Plastic is almost indestructible. Most of the plastic manufactured is still around. Recycling plastic is a way to help the environment.

CHAPTER THREE

Nuclear Meltdown

Nuclear reactors use **fission** to create energy for power. Fission takes place when the nucleus of an atom is hit by a fast moving atomic particle called a neutron. This collision breaks the nucleus into smaller parts, releasing heat energy and other particles. In nuclear reactors, this energy is controlled and used to produce electricity. The particles from fuel send off **radiation**, or energy, that can penetrate matter. Some materials give off radiation naturally. Uranium, a reactor fuel, is a radioactive element.

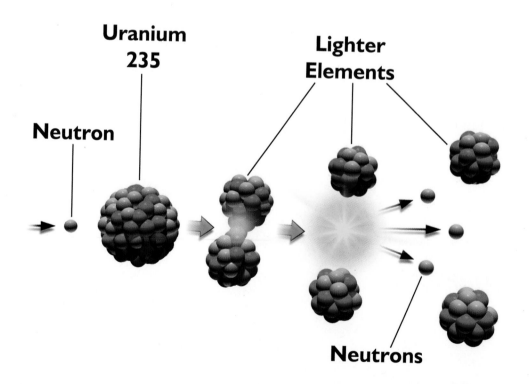

Uranium 235

Lighter Elements

Neutron

Neutrons

High levels of radiation can escape in an uncontrolled nuclear reaction. Radiation contaminates air and water for hundreds of miles. High levels of radiation sicken or kill living things. Radiation damages cells or alters people's DNA. Cell changes can cause cancer. People will die if too much tissue and organ damage occurs.

On March 28, 1979, an uncontrolled nuclear meltdown happened in a reactor accident at Three Mile Island, Pennsylvania. A series of errors led to the failures that caused it.

The clean-up of the damaged Three Mile Island reactor Unit 2 took almost twelve years to complete. The damaged uranium fuel was safely removed and stored in concrete containers in Idaho.

NEW YORK

PENNSYLVANIA

Three Mile Island

MARYLAND

WEST VIRGINIA

At Three Mile Island, operators unclogging a steam pipe accidentally blocked the flow of water that cooled the reactor. The core heated the water and raised the pressure. A valve opened to let off extra pressure. The heat increased and fission continued without cool water. Control rods dropped into the reactor to stop the fission chain reaction. The valve should have closed. But it didn't—it was stuck open. The reactor lost its cooling water as steam poured out.

The valve appeared closed to the operator. He turned off the water pump. The remaining water boiled away from the heat of the radioactive fuel. Radiation levels rose. The fuel rods ruptured.

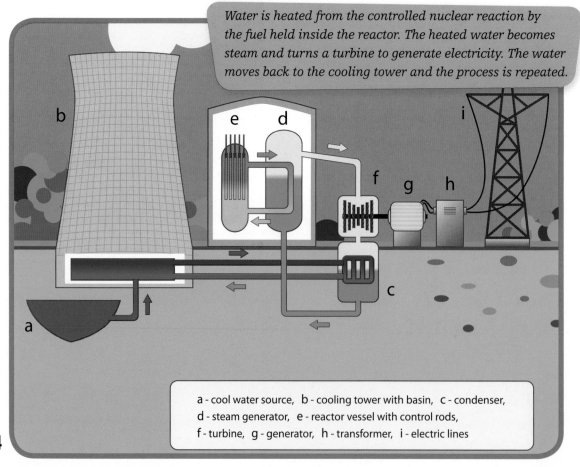

Water is heated from the controlled nuclear reaction by the fuel held inside the reactor. The heated water becomes steam and turns a turbine to generate electricity. The water moves back to the cooling tower and the process is repeated.

a - cool water source, b - cooling tower with basin, c - condenser,
d - steam generator, e - reactor vessel with control rods,
f - turbine, g - generator, h - transformer, i - electric lines

The operator did close the valve. But he didn't add more water. He did later, but the water couldn't reach the collapsed fuel rods inside. No one knew the core had melted into the bottom of the reactor. The container wasn't made to hold such hot, radioactive material. Fortunately, the container held. Water slowly cooled the core, but high radiation levels concerned everyone. The Nuclear Regulation Commission (NRC) declared an emergency.

People worried about radiation exposure, but levels remained normal. However, the reactor had to be dismantled. Cleanup and **decontamination** wasn't finished until 1993 and cost $975 million. Many people opposed nuclear energy and raised concerns about its use.

Workers wear protective clothing, headgear, shoe covers, respirators, and gloves to clean up nuclear wastes. Mops, brooms, and high pressure washes are used to decontaminate high-level nuclear waste.

On the left is the now shut down reactor Unit 2. It is still monitored regularly. Today, reactor Unit 1 continues to generate power. It will continue until the license expires. The company will then close down, or decommission, that reactor.

The NRC tightened controls over reactor regulations and safety. Changes in emergency response, engineering, training, inspections, and management took place. Fortunately the disaster inside didn't cause a disaster outside the reactor.

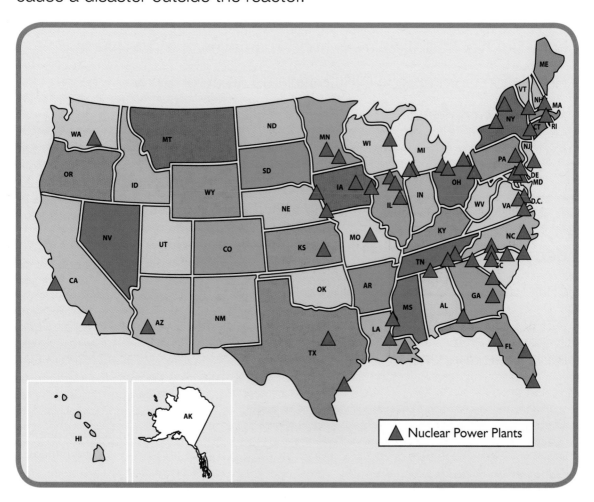

While the Three Mile Island accident didn't kill anyone, that wasn't the case in Chernobyl in the Ukraine. That meltdown happened on April 26, 1986.

Human error and poor design caused the Chernobyl accident. The old Soviet-designed reactor used graphite and water for heat control. Without approval, operators ran the plant

at low power. This caused a power surge in the reactor. The fuel tubes ruptured. Hot fuel hit the water and exploded. The reactor's top blew off and burst the other fuel tubes. The open core sat and burned for ten days.

Twenty years after the nuclear meltdown, little has changed at the Chernobyl reactor site. Time reduces the levels of radiation as it breaks down naturally, although some of the fuels take thousands of years to become entirely safe.

Twenty-eight recovery and cleanup workers died from radiation and burns. Nineteen others died later. Thousands developed thyroid cancer from radiation. Although not considered at toxic levels, radiation carried by wind and rain spread across Europe and England. In fact, radiation even reached the United States.

Operators tried to cover up the accident. Soviet leaders evacuated people thirty-six hours later. By May, 1986, over 116,000 people had to leave their homes. Radiation entered the groundwater and moved through the food chain. The radiation left in the meltdown area could last for at least 1,000 years.

Most people left their homes and never returned. Today, a few people have returned home by choice, but radiation levels are above normal. However, these levels are not considered fatal.

Radiation levels can be measured by a geiger counter.

This abandoned kindergarten classroom provides a picture of the long ago, sudden exit and tragedy for the families of Pripyat. Most of them will never return.

Today, a 17 mile (27 kilometers) perimeter around the plant remains the exclusion zone. Tours visit the site today. Some radiation still lingers, but exposure is at acceptable levels for a short time. New regulations and reactors are used now.

In 2011, a powerful earthquake and tsunami hit the coast of Japan. The tsunami knocked out the electricity running the cooling systems of the nuclear reactors. The reactors overheated and backup systems lost power. Explosions rocked the reactors. Three of the nuclear reactors melted down and radiation was released in the area.

Nuclear power is useful, but the public must remain safe.

Could a Chernobyl accident happen here?

Four differences keep the U.S. from having a Chernobyl-like meltdown. New technology and regulations make nuclear facilities safer. Many more safety features are built into the U.S. reactors. They have emergency plans ready if a problem occurs. The public must be notified within fifteen minutes of a problem. Resident inspectors are posted at every plant. These plans are to keep the public safe.

CHAPTER FOUR

Acid Rain

A **pH** scale is a way to show how acidic or basic substances are. The scale ranges from zero to fourteen, with seven being neutral. A pH less than seven is acidic. Substances nearer zero are more acidic. Each number lower is ten times more acidic. Vinegar and lemon juice are acids.

A pH higher than seven indicates a base. Each number is ten times more basic, or **alkaline**. Strong bases are closer to fourteen. Washing detergent and ammonia are bases.

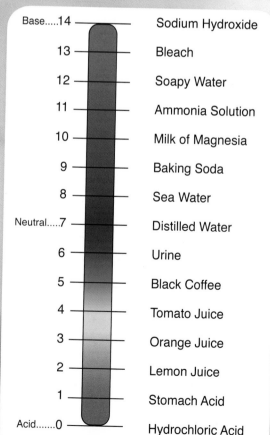

Base.....14	Sodium Hydroxide
13	Bleach
12	Soapy Water
11	Ammonia Solution
10	Milk of Magnesia
9	Baking Soda
8	Sea Water
Neutral.....7	Distilled Water
6	Urine
5	Black Coffee
4	Tomato Juice
3	Orange Juice
2	Lemon Juice
1	Stomach Acid
Acid.......0	Hydrochloric Acid

Pure water is neutral. Normal rain contains dissolved carbon dioxide, making it a weak acid. Its normal pH is about 5.6. Other gases can dissolve in rainwater, too. If they are acidic, it makes **acid rain**.

Acid rain, or acid deposition, comes from acidic gases in the air. Nitric and sulfuric acids are the most common. Some of them come from volcanoes or decaying vegetation. Most of them come from human sources.

Burning fossil fuel makes **emissions** of sulfur dioxides and nitrogen oxide. Power plants burning coal create the most emissions. The Sun's energy causes a chemical reaction in the emissions using oxygen and water in the air. This makes mild nitric and sulfuric acids. The acidic gases attach to drops of water, snow, mists, or dry dust in the air. Once they land, they are deposited.

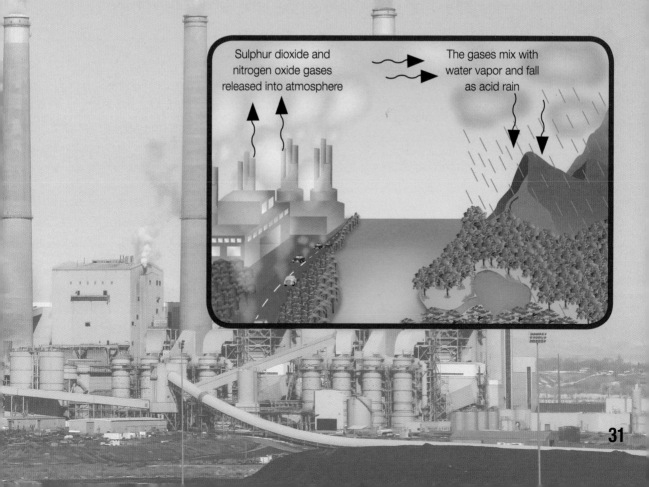

Sulphur dioxide and nitrogen oxide gases released into atmosphere

The gases mix with water vapor and fall as acid rain

Acid rain looks and feels like normal rain. For a long time, people didn't know it existed. In the 1960s, scientists found the water in northeastern lakes more acidic than normal. They noticed that emissions from burning coal in Indiana, Ohio, Kentucky, and Illinois blew toward the northeastern U.S. and Canada. Acid rain fell in the lakes.

The worst damage from acid rain in the U.S occurred in the northeast. Scientists measuring acidity in lakes found over half the lakes tested high for acid. In the 1970s, half of the lakes there had such high levels of acid that fish and other animals died. By the 1970s and 1980s, pH levels went as low at 2.1, or about 1,000 times the normal acidity level. Ten years later, half of the lakes had little or no life in them.

Rainbow trout, smallmouth bass, minnows, clams, snails, and mayflies can't survive in a pH lower than 5.5. As they die, organisms depending on them as food die out, too. The food chain ends.

Acid rain weakens trees over time. The acids pull aluminum from the soil and rocks. Aluminum destroys root hairs of trees and they can't get water and nutrients. Stressed trees are then killed by cold, drought, insects, and diseases.

The Adirondack Mountains especially suffered. Soils containing the mineral calcium carbonate can neutralize acids before they get into the lakes. But the Adirondacks have very little of this mineral. Increased damage happened to the waterways. Streams and ponds provide habitats for different **organisms**. Besides killing life in the water and upsetting the food chain, acid rain damages tree leaves. They can't carry out photosynthesis. Stressed trees suffered.

The acids damage the soil, too. Plants need calcium to live. Acids leach calcium from the soil. Tree needles thin and can't resist the cold as well.

33

Acidic gases limit visibility in the Shenandoah area and Great Smoky Mountains. Acid rain wears away monuments, statues, and memorials. It harms building materials and paints. The pollutants causing acid rain harm human health. They contribute to lung disorders like asthma, bronchitis, and other breathing problems. Concerns grew over acid rain and the environment.

Fighting began among environmentalists, scientists, and power plant owners. People called for laws to change but power plants worried they'd lose money. People weren't sure laws would improve the environment.

Pitted limestone on this building shows the damage acid rain can cause in a relatively short time. Limestone and marble are made of calcite, which acids can easily dissolve. Drop chalk in a cup of vinegar to see how this happens.

What Can You Do?

People can reduce energy use, save money, and help the environment. Small changes make a big difference when everybody does them. Try these tips for helping the environment:

1. Walk or bike.
2. Use public transportation or carpool.
3. Use energy efficient lights and appliances.
4. Turn off lights, TVs, and computers when you aren't using them.
5. Set thermostats to 68 degrees in winter and 78 degrees in summer.
6. Save hot chores for the coolest time of day.

Canada

United States

Adirondack Mountains

New York

Pennsylvania

Maryland

West Virginia

Shenandoah

Virginia

Kentucky

North Carolina

Tennessee

Great Smoky Mountains

South Carolina

Georgia

Congress passed the Clean Air Act in 1970. They added acid deposition controls in 1990. The Acid Rain Program reduced emissions. By 2000, the pH of acid rain was 4.3. Some effects of acid rain remain, but most scientists agree it's a successful clean-up of the environment.

Acid rain affects everyone. What people do in one place affects the environment in another. Everyone has a responsibility to keep the Earth safe.

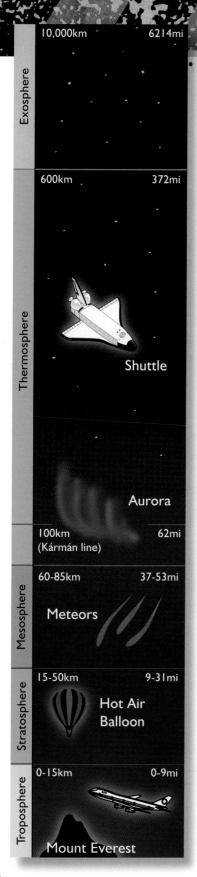

Exosphere

10,000km   6214mi

600km   372mi

Thermosphere

Shuttle

Aurora

100km   62mi
(Kármán line)

Mesosphere

60-85km   37-53mi

Meteors

Stratosphere

15-50km   9-31mi

Hot Air
Balloon

Troposphere

0-15km   0-9mi

Mount Everest

CHAPTER FIVE

Hole in the Ozone

The atmosphere is a layer of gases surrounding Earth. It extends 372 miles (600 km) upward. The atmosphere absorbs the Sun's energy, provides our livable climate, and contains the water cycle. It is made of four major zones.

The **troposphere** extends about 9 miles (15 km) high. Most weather occurs in this layer. The temperature decreases with altitude. The **stratosphere** is the next layer. It extends about 31 miles (50 km). A layer of **ozone**, or molecules made of three oxygen atoms, is in this part of the atmosphere. Ozone absorbs and scatters the Sun's **ultraviolet** (UV) energy. This helpful ozone keeps too much of the UV radiation from hitting Earth. It also holds in the right amount of heat for life on Earth.

In the 1980s, atmospheric scientists found a large hole in the ozone layer over Antarctica. They feared the hole was growing. More UV radiation could enter the atmosphere. Too much radiation would cause eye damage, sunburn, and even skin cancer. It harms the immune system. Radiation changes the ocean's chemistry, too, creating harmful compounds. Scientists wanted to find out what caused the hole in the ozone.

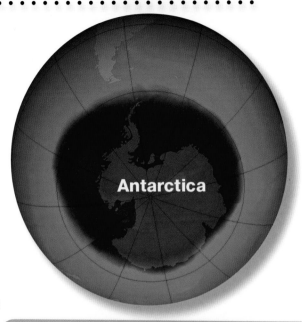

Images from NASA show the ozone hole in 2009. The blue and purple colors are where there is the least ozone, and the green is where there is more ozone.

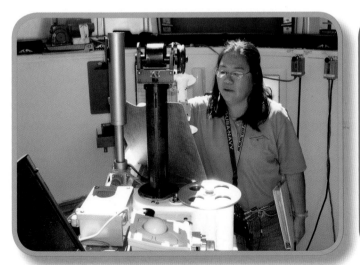 

Measuring the ozone layer allows scientists to track changes taking place each year. The Dobson spectrophotometer on the right, first built in the 1920s, measures changes in an ozone column by comparing ultraviolet (UV) light absorption with the Sun or Moon as a light source.

Protective ozone is in a balance. Oxygen gas is made of two atoms of oxygen bonded together. High energy UV light hits the oxygen molecule. It splits into two unstable oxygen atoms. Unstable oxygen needs to bond to something. The free oxygen atoms hit other paired oxygen molecules and attach to them. Adding a third oxygen atom makes ozone.

At the same time, ozone absorbs UV light. The light energy splits the ozone molecule apart. This makes the paired oxygen molecule and a free oxygen atom. By absorbing the energy, the ozone protects the Earth.

Studies showed **chlorofluorocarbons** (CFCs), a compound containing chlorine atoms, caused ozone reduction. CFCs, like Freon for refrigeration and for making foam and soaps and the spray in spray cans are not toxic to humans but they are toxic to the atmosphere. CFCs are not toxic to people.

CFCs cause great environmental damage when wind blows them into the stratosphere. There, UV radiation splits them and the free chlorine breaks apart ozone. Each chlorine atom destroys huge amounts of ozone. Broken down CFCs added chlorine atoms, thus reducing ozone levels. CFCs last in the atmosphere between twenty and one hundred years. Pesticides and other chemicals destroy ozone, too.

NOAA and NASA say the average temperature of the Earth's surface has increased by about a degree since 1900 because of human activities. Storms and rainfall are affected by the temperature change, too.

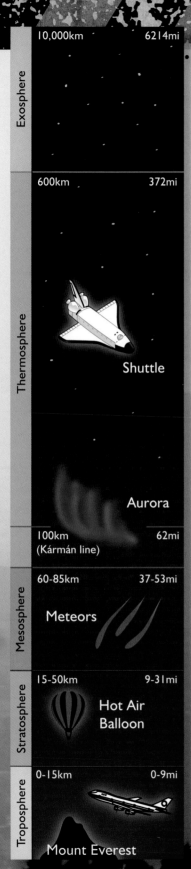

Countries came together and agreed to stop producing CFCs. The Montreal Protocol called for a stop to CFCs. Reducing CFCs gives the ozone time to repair itself. Chlorine in the stratosphere slowed and then reversed. Scientists predict by 2065 ozone should return to the levels of the 1980s. Until then, UV radiation will be higher than normal.

Troposphere ozone is harmful. It keeps heat from leaving the atmosphere. Ozone dirties the air, contributes to smog, and causes health problems. It's toxic to living things. It attracts oxygen atoms from plants and people. This harms lungs and upsets the balance of gases in plants.

Smog today means a decrease in air quality that affects visibility or human health. It develops when emissions are trapped by the local weather and becomes concentrated. Chemical reactions often take place in smog.

Ground level ozone is formed when nitrogen oxides and other unstable compounds react in the air using the Sun's energy. Car and industrial emissions, gasoline vapors, and other chemicals give off these compounds. Hot summer temperatures increase ground ozone levels.

The buildup of extra heat-trapping gases in the atmosphere has warmed the Earth. These gases are called greenhouse gases. They trap the heat and hold it so it can't escape. Global warming is causing polar ice caps and glaciers to melt. Rising sea levels threaten coastlines. Eliminating greenhouse gases helps reduce harmful air pollution.

Some toxic compounds are present in gasoline and move into the air when the engine burns gas to run or as gas evaporates. Some unburned fuel also moves into the air. Improving fuel, emissions controls, and alternative fuels are important for improving air quality.

Solar energy from the Sun passes through the atmosphere.

Earth's surface is heated by the Sun and radiates the heat back out toward space.

atmosphere

Some energy is reflected back out to space.

Greenhouse gases in the atmosphere trap some of the heat.

GREENHOUSE GASES

Ozone creates changes in temperature. More ozone retains more heat. The stratosphere has cooled while the Earth's climate has warmed. Scientists are looking for a link between these two events.

Other climate factors influence ozone formation. Future space missions and new satellites will help everyone better understand the links between ozone and climate.

Even a small temperature rise will melt glaciers and the polar ice. Animals depending on the ice must find new ways to get food or they face extinction.

43

Sunburned Whales

A new research study has scientists looking at blue whales, fin whales, and sperm whales with skin damage in the Gulf of California. For years, researchers noticed blisters on the skin of these whales that looked like sunburn seen on humans. They found more damage in the lighter-skinned whales. As whales come to the surface to breathe they are exposed to the rising levels of UV radiation. Scientists suspect ozone depletion or changes in the cloud cover. They will continue the study to learn more.

People change the environment to suit their purposes, but often harmful results happen. Building levees in locations below sea level invites breaching and flooding disasters like the one in New Orleans following hurricane Katrina. Cutting down trees for fuel in Haiti eroded the soil. Fires, caused by humans, have burned forests in Yellowstone and elsewhere.

Hurricane Katrina pounded the city of New Orleans, but the flooding damage resulted from the levees not holding back the incoming high sea water.

Oil, chemicals, nuclear power, and emissions all come from progress. Human activities will continue to change the environment. The kinds of changes people make today will determine the future of their environment.

Toxic waste pollutes the waterways, but it doesn't always kill an animal outright. Sometimes the effects cause genetic mutations, which results in abnormal or ill young.

Glossary

acid rain (ASS-id rayn): rainwater containing acidic gases like nitric or sulfuric acid

alkaline (AL-kuh-line): a substance on the base side of the pH scale

berms (burmz): physical barriers formed by piling up stacks of material

bioremediation (bye-oh-ri-MEE-dee-ay-shuhn): using naturally occurring microbes to clean up environmental problems

carcinogens (kahr-SIN-oh-jinz): cancer-causing agents

chlorofluorocarbons (KLOR-oh-flor-oh-kahr-buhnz): compounds that give up fluorine atoms easily

decontamination (dee-kuhn-TAM-uh-nay-shun): removal or clean-up of harmful or toxic material

dispersants (dis-PURS-uhntss): materials that scatter or break apart substances into smaller particles

emissions (i-MISH-uhnz): waste given off, usually by combustion or some form of burning

e-waste (EE-wayst): discarded technology appliances or tools

fission (FISH-uhn:) the splitting of an atom's nucleus

gyre (jire): the area in an ocean where currents meet up and slowly swirl in a circular motion

ingests (in-JESTSS): to take in by mouth and swallow

organisms (OR-guh-niz-uhmz): any living forms of life

ozone (OH-zone): a molecule of oxygen made of three atoms of oxygen

pH (pee- aych): a measure of how acidic or alkaline a substance is

radiation (ray-dee-AY-shuhn): atomic particles coming from a radioactive material

stratosphere (STRAT-uh-sfihr): the layer of the Earth's atmosphere beginning about nine miles high which contains the protective ozone layer

troposphere (TROH-po-sfihr): the layer of the Earth's atmosphere nearest the ground and where weather occurs

ultraviolet (uhl-truh-VYE-uh-lit): a type of radiation that can't be seen and can cause skin to tan or burn

Index

Wesites to Visit

www.epa.gov/acidrain/education/site_students/index.html

www.sunshine.chpc.utah.edu/labs/ozone/ozone_main.html

www.eia.doe.gov/kids/energy.cfm?page=nuclear_home-basics

www.nwf.org/Kids/Ranger-Rick/People-and-Places/Ranger-Rick-on-the-Big-Oil-Spill.
aspx

www.epa.gov/climatechange/kids/index.html

About the Author

Shirley Duke enjoys science and books. She studied biology and education at Austin College in Texas. Then she taught science in elementary, middle, and high school for many years. Using her science background, she changed careers and now writes books for young people. She's written a picture book and a young adult book, but her first two science books are You Can't Wear These Genes and Infections, Infestations, and Diseases in the "Let's Explore Science" series. Visit Shirley at www.shirleysmithduke.com or www.simplyscience.wordpress.com.